International Labour Office

LABOUR INSPECTION POLICY AND PLANNING

A practical guide

Robert Heron
Henrik Vistisen
Kazuo Yamazaki

ILO East Asia Multidisciplinary Advisory Team
ILO Regional Office for Asia and the Pacific
Bangkok

First published 1998

ISBN 92-2-111280-2

For information on how to obtain this publication write to the ILO East Asia Multidisciplinary Advisory Team, P.O. Box 2-349, Rajdamnern Avenue, Bangkok 10200, Thailand. Catalogues and lists of recent and forthcoming ILO books are available free of charge from the ILO Regional Office for Asia and the Pacific, 11th Floor, United Nations Building, Rajdamnern Avenue, Bangkok 10200; fax (66-2) 280-1735, 281-1496.

Printed in Thailand

Foreword

Labour inspectors need to have access to training materials and guides in developing labour inspection services. The main target group for this guide is senior labour inspectors responsible for shaping policy, formulating enforcement strategies, and planning labour inspection activities.

The guide is presented in simple terms, avoids technical language, and highlights key points for easy reference. It is sufficiently comprehensive to help senior officials in their day-to-day activities, and also provides a framework for training newly appointed labour inspectors.

The booklet is designed as a training tool for labour inspectorates which lack the means to conduct training for labour inspectors and have limited training materials to support the training they can conduct. It is also intended to motivate the managers of labour inspection services to rethink their roles and adopt more innovative approaches in providing inspection services.

The guide can be used for both group training and self-learning. It will be particularly useful for senior labour inspectors in provinces and districts where access to training and staff development is limited compared with opportunities for headquarters personnel.

Translation of the guide into national languages is encouraged, as are comments and suggestions for improvement from its users.

The guide has been prepared by Robert Heron, Senior Labour Administration Specialist, Kazuo Yamazaki, former Japan International Cooperation Agency Expert on Labour Inspection, and Henrik Vistisen, Associate Expert in Labour Administration, of the ILO East Asia Multidisciplinary Advisory Team.

W. R. Simpson
Director
ILO East Asia Multidisciplinary
Advisory Team (ILO/EASMAT)

Bangkok
June 1998

Table of contents

Introduction

An increasing number of products from more and more countries are entering world markets, requiring enterprises to reduce costs to maintain a competitive edge. In such circumstances, labour standards to protect workers, and their enforcement, are sometimes considered an obstacle to greater efficiency. Government interventions in the interest of labour protection are seen as distortions in free-market operation, resulting in higher wages and non-wage labour costs, thereby limiting opportunities to compete in global markets. Accepting this argument would mean virtually abolishing labour inspection services, with free-market forces undermining social protection.

Concurrent with increased global competition is the trend towards greater liberalization in countries in transition from central planning to a free-market environment where resource allocation is more and more influenced by market forces. The desire to attract investment and create employment in line with economic imperatives can dominate the social imperative of labour protection. As with globalization, increased liberalization puts pressure on governments to reduce their interventions in the labour market, with the need for labour inspection services being further questioned and opposed.

But any attempt to marginalize labour inspection work must be resisted. Globalization and liberalization place increased pressure on labour resources, requiring greater vigilance by labour inspectorates if labour exploitation and deteriorating working conditions are to be avoided. The modalities of labour protection interventions may have to change, but their purpose and objectives remain the same.

This chapter emphasizes that labour inspection activities are fundamental to social justice and provide important services for both workers and employers. It covers a range of policy and planning aspects of concern to labour inspectorates.

Chapter 2 discusses the key aspects of inspection and emphasizes the need for law enforcement priorities. Special attention is given to the many difficult, and sometimes contrasting, roles of labour inspectors, and how labour inspectorates' powers are moderated by a series of obligations.

Chapter 3 focuses on planning inspectorates' activities according to priorities, needs, and available resources. The planning process emphasizes action planning, with examples of work programmes.

Chapter 4 considers a range of policy issues. It highlights the relationship between labour inspection and industrial relations, and between labour inspection and factory inspection. It examines the functions and structure of labour inspectorates, stressing the need to enhance their productivity and efficiency. It discusses new trends and approaches in labour inspection in the light of technological and social developments.

The very important question of how to extend labour inspection coverage is also dealt with in this chapter. It outlines the financial constraints imposed on inspectorates, and proposes ways to mobilize new resources and make better use of existing ones. It considers the possible role of the social partners – employers and workers – and the active use of the mass media by inspectorates.

The text of the ILO Labour Inspection Convention, 1947 (No. 81), and the ILO Labour Inspection Recommendation, 1947 (No. 81), is in the annex.

This guide is complemented by a companion guide, *Conducting labour inspection visits: A practical guide.*

2 What is labour inspection?

A. Functions of labour inspectors

Labour inspectors:

- enforce the labour law and related regulations
- advise employers and workers on how to comply with the law
- report to superiors on problems and defects not covered by the law.

In some countries inspectors perform other functions, including:

- promoting harmonious relations between employers and workers
- investigating, conciliating, and mediating disputes between employers and workers.

Labour inspectors are part of the government machinery, and their essential purpose is to develop labour and social relations in an orderly way.

B. Enforcing the labour law

Inspectors enforce the law concerning:

- the terms and conditions of work, including wages, hours, leave, and overtime payment
- workplace safety and health
- the employment of children, young persons, and women.

The scope of their enforcement powers differs according to national circumstances. In some countries certain categories of workers are excluded from the law, including:

- domestic workers
- homeworkers
- farm workers.

Efforts should be made to extend labour inspection services to all workplaces and all workers and employers.

C. Informing and advising on the law

Inspectors' duties of informing and advising employers **and** workers include:

- explaining what the law means
- indicating where legal requirements are not met
- explaining what needs to be done to comply with the law.

In giving advice inspectors concentrate on what requires to be done rather than how to do it.

Example:

An inspector may detect that the dust level in a factory is too high and advises the employer to install an exhaust system. But it is not the inspector's task to design the system and supervise its installation.

In advising on how to comply with the law, inspectors have to take decisions to the best of their judgement.

Examples:

How much time should the inspector allow the employer to install an exhaust system to eliminate the dust problem?

How much time should the inspector allow the employer to make back payments where wages have been under-paid?

Inspectorates should consider how to provide information on the law to the wider community.

D. Problems not covered by the law

In the course of their duties inspectors will find problems not covered by the law. These should be:

- identified
- described and explained
- reported to senior labour officials.

Problems not covered by the law would normally be included in the inspection visit report.

Reported defects can be used as a basis for amending the law.

Inspectors have an important role in improving social and labour legislation.

E. Powers of inspectors

Power is the ability to influence others.

For effective performance, inspectors need to exercise three different, but related, forms of power:

- position power
- technical power
- person power.

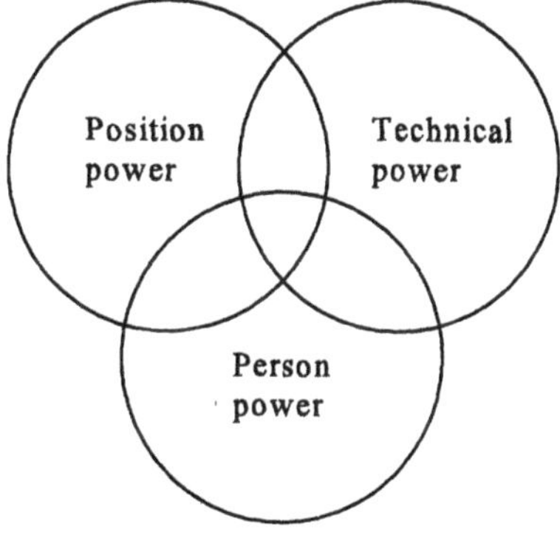

1. Position power

Position power is the formal power derived from an official or generally recognized source.

Inspectors' position power is conferred by:

- the labour law and regulations
- letters of appointment
- assigned duties and responsibilities in formal job descriptions.

Position power, in itself, is not sufficient to guarantee compliance with the law.

Evidence of inspectors' position power is usually provided by a special identity card.

Inspectors' position power is important but, in itself, is not sufficient to ensure compliance with the law.

Powers accorded to inspectors by their **position** include to:

- freely enter workplaces liable to inspection (those defined by the law and usually registered)
- enter workplaces without appointment
- enter premises which they have reasonable cause to believe are liable to inspection (those within the legal definition but usually unregistered)
- carry out any examination, test, or enquiry to determine whether the law is being observed
- interview the employer and workers
- examine books, registers, and documents relating to working conditions
- copy any document
- enforce the posting of notices required by the law
- take samples of materials and substances, provided the employer is notified
- take steps to remedy defects which they have reasonable cause to believe are a threat to workers' safety and health
- issue orders requiring alterations to the plant or installation

- issue orders with immediate effect if there is imminent danger to workers' safety and health

- initiate legal proceedings against the employer

- require the official notification of industrial accidents and industrial diseases.

2. *Technical power*

Technical power is a combination of the knowledge, skills, and accumulated experience of inspectors.

Technical power includes:

- detailed knowledge of the labour law and regulations
- the ability to advise on how to comply with the law
- technical knowledge in specialized areas, such as engineering, chemistry, and industrial sociology
- knowledge of economics and industrial relations
- knowledge of human relations and interaction
- the ability to analyse financial records
- the ability to analyse work processes and identify problems.

3. Person power

A combination of position power and technical power is essential for effective inspection. But this is not enough. Effective inspection also requires person power.

Person power refers to the way inspectors **use** their position power and technical power.

Person power includes the ability to:

- relate to other people
- motivate and persuade people
- gain the confidence and cooperation of others
- avoid and resolve conflict situations.

The essential skill in inspection work is finding a suitable balance between position power, technical power, and person power.

F. Obligations of inspectors

Giving powers to inspectors does not mean they can do whatever they wish. Their powers must be moderated by a series of obligations.

Inspectors should:

- notify employers of their presence when on inspection visits (This does **not** mean that inspectors must give advance notice of all visits.)
- undertake not to reveal any secret processes and information which may harm employers' competitive position
- keep confidential the source of complaints against employers
- show their labour inspection identity card to employers
- submit periodic reports to superiors
- be independent and impartial
- have no direct or indirect interest in the enterprises under their supervision.

Labour inspectors have obligations as well as rights and powers.

3 Planning inspection

A. The importance of planning

Labour inspectorates' work should be properly planned if policy objectives and obligations under the labour law are to be met.

Policy directives, to be effective, require to be translated into action plans.

Law enforcement should be systematically planned if the best use is to be made of the scarce resources available to inspectorates.

Planning should not be seen as something that **might** be done if time allows.

Planning is of fundamental importance if inspectorates are to improve their overall performance.

Planning is not merely desirable, it is essential.

B. What is planning?

Planning is the bridge between the present and the future.

Planning involves preparing for action at some future point in time – the next day, next week, next month, next year.

Planning is the opposite of chaos and crisis. It attempts to transform chaos into order and reduce uncertainty to a more manageable level.

Planning requires considering priorities.

Planning is a tool to transform the possible into reality.

Resources are scarce; through good planning it is possible to establish priorities for their effective use.

C. The planning process

Planning involves:

- taking stock of the existing situation
- establishing a broad vision of the future
- setting objectives for achieving the vision
- fixing targets reflecting the results to be achieved
- setting standards indicating the quality of outputs to be achieved
- relating objectives and targets to a definite time-frame
- comparing **expected** costs and benefits **before** implementing the plan
- considering monitoring arrangements when implementing the plan
- considering the evaluation arrangements required at the end of the plan period.

Planning entails **action strategies** to ensure objectives, targets, and standards are achieved.

When making plans it is crucial that all concerned are clear about their responsibilities and the time-frame.

D. Action planning

Action planning involves deciding who will do what and when.

Before inspectorates prepare detailed action plans the following questions must be addressed:

- What is the legal definition of an enterprise?
- How many enterprises are liable to inspection under the definition?
- Is it necessary to inspect **all** enterprises legally liable to inspection?
- How frequently should enterprises liable to inspection be visited?

  Example:

Objective:	To inspect all joint-venture enterprises, totalling 1,250, twice during the next year.
Inspectors:	50
Number of visits required:	1,250 x 2 times a year = 2,500
Target per inspector:	50 inspections a year or about four a month

  If it is decided that inspectors will work in teams of two, each team will conduct 100 visits a year, or each inspector will undertake approximately eight visits a month.

- Where are the enterprises liable to inspection located?
- Which enterprises liable to inspection should be given priority?
- How should priorities be determined? [by size, location, type of ownership (e.g. private or public company, partnership, state-owned enterprise), degree of risk]

- How many active inspectors are there to undertake inspection work?

- What is a reasonable number of monthly inspections for each inspector?

- Will inspectors work in teams or alone?

Once responses to these questions are available it will be possible to develop a detailed work programme for each inspectorate and each inspector.

E. Work programmes

Each inspector's work programme will require to be prepared based on the labour inspectorate's action plan.

Each inspector should know which enterprises to inspect weekly and monthly, and how often.

Each inspector's work programme must take account of his or her duties, as well as public holidays and annual leave.

Individual work programmes should provide time for crisis situations.

Individual work programmes should be prepared in consultation with inspectors, superiors, and colleagues.

The individual work programme is an important tool to monitor and evaluate the inspector's performance on an ongoing basis.

4 Policy issues

Labour inspectorates should consider a range of policy issues likely to have an impact on their future role, structure, and organizational arrangements. These include:

- labour inspection and industrial relations
- labour inspection and factory inspection
- the organization of labour, safety, and health inspectorates
- new approaches to inspection
- the productivity of labour inspectorates
- technological developments
- new work arrangements
- homeworkers
- extension of inspection coverage.

A. Labour inspection and industrial relations

Integrating labour inspection functions with industrial relations functions requires a clear understanding of the nature of each function.

Labour inspection **concerns enforcing labour protection laws, and advising employers and workers on how to comply with legal provisions.**

Industrial relations **concerns the interaction between workers, employers, and the government relating to work or arising out of the workplace.**

The interaction between workers and employers, and government intervention which influences the interaction clearly touch on matters of labour inspection.

Example:

Minimum wage regulations stipulate pay rates for workers. Pay rates are checked by inspectors as part of their routine inspection functions.

If there is a discrepancy between the wage paid and the minimum entitlement, the inspector must instruct the employer to comply with the law.

If the employer refuses, there is an individual rights dispute between the worker and the employer, and a breach of the law.

Who should handle this problem? Should it be taken up immediately by the labour inspector or should it be referred to a specialist industrial relations officer?

Individual **rights disputes**, which concern the **existing** terms and conditions of employment, can be resolved informally by labour inspectors.

Labour inspectors can often solve labour problems at their first point of contact.

Interest disputes, which concern the future terms and conditions of employment, are better handled by specialist industrial relations officers.

***Rights disputes* are disputes over the existing terms and conditions of employment.**

***Interest disputes* are disputes over the future terms and conditions of employment.**

A department of labour with sufficient resources may separate labour inspection functions and industrial relations functions, and appoint specialist officers for each function. Where resources are scarce, it may be necessary to combine these functions and appoint generalist labour officers.

Labour inspectorates are seen as the front line of labour ministries, and should be well informed about all ministry functions.

B. Labour inspection and factory inspection

In some countries inspection functions are separated:

- inspection of the terms and conditions of employment (labour inspection)
- inspection of safety and health (factory inspection).

In other countries labour inspection functions and factory inspection functions are integrated under **one** labour inspectorate.

***Factory inspection* is the inspection of workplace safety and health.**

***Labour inspection* is the inspection of the terms and conditions of employment.**

ILO Convention No. 81 states that labour inspection is concerned with **both:**

- the terms and conditions of employment (hours, wages, holidays)
- the working environment (safety and health).

C. The organization of labour, safety, and health inspectorates

Most developing countries have separate inspectorates as line departments within the same ministry.

In developing countries inspection services are typically divided between:

- a labour inspectorate responsible for the terms and conditions of employment (wages, hours, maternity benefits, overtime, child workers)
- a safety inspectorate in charge of work safety (machine guarding, materials handling, chemical storage)
- a health inspectorate responsible for occupational health and work-related diseases.

Such services involve different specializations:

- Labour inspectorates, ideally, have labour specialists from a variety of educational backgrounds.
- Safety inspectorates have engineers, chemists, and other professionals with a technical background.
- Health inspectorates have medical professionals.

In countries with limited resources for inspection, generalist labour inspectors should be involved in safety and health inspection. This would mean retraining generalist labour inspectors or, in the longer term, recruiting all inspectors with some technical qualifications.

General inspection reports should highlight:

- areas requiring follow-up by specialist inspectors
- matters where generalist labour inspectors consider that a particular problem is beyond their competence.

  Example:

  A generalist labour inspector undertakes routine factory inspection. The inspector discovers a problem relating to the use of chemicals and reports it to a safety inspector, who makes a specialized inspection the next day.

  The safety inspector will concentrate on specific problems rather than the routine matters already dealt with by the generalist labour inspector.

One approach to organizing inspection activities is to **integrate** the work of labour inspectors and factory inspectors. Under this approach:

- most of the inspection work is done by generalist labour inspectors
- generalist labour inspectors are supported by a team of technical specialists
- technical specialists could be engaged as consultants rather than full-time employees.

An integrated approach to inspection has these advantages:

- better use of resources
- improved relations between the inspectorate and clients
- more focused use of specialist staff resources.

If an integrated approach to inspection is not possible, labour, safety, and health inspectorates must cooperate through:

- regular consultations
- joint training activities
- exchange of reports
- team inspections.

The purpose of inspection is to enforce the labour law, ensure compliance with legal provisions, and identify defects in the law. As a result, the workplace will become more healthy and productive, benefiting workers and employers. Organizational and structural arrangements for inspection services should respond to this objective alone.

D. New approaches to inspection

Changes in work arrangements and the speed at which they occur require different approaches to inspection work.

Example:

There is increasing emphasis on providing specialist services to enterprises (e.g. medical) and greater reliance on safety and health committees and works committees, which bring employers and workers closer to complying with the labour law and regulations. This is both a challenge and an opportunity:

- a challenge because inspectors need to consult a large number of institutions

- an opportunity as these institutions can be used to promote and enhance inspectors' work.

As enterprises develop, become more dynamic, and take more initiative, the labour inspectorate becomes part of a process of facilitating change rather than engaging only in traditional inspection activities.

Greater emphasis is now placed on:

- the development of labour protection policies at the workplace

- prevention rather than cure.

This makes the work of inspectors more difficult and complex because they must have detailed knowledge of:

- the business operations of an enterprise
- social relations within the enterprise
- the structure and procedures of the enterprise.

The purpose of inspection is no longer limited to promoting compliance with the law. Modern inspection approaches promote *social relations* between workers and management.

Under the preventive approach, inspectorates acquire legitimacy through:

- competence
- efficiency
- technical power
- person power.

A preventive approach to labour inspection requires an inspector to be more an adviser than an enforcer.

The preventive approach has three main consequences:

- Inspectors deal more with **top** management and workers' representatives.
- Inspectors **advise** management rather than do management's job.
- Inspectors are **better trained** to have a good understanding of the management process and labour relations.

Under a preventive approach to labour inspection, inspection services rely on technical power and person power rather than on position power.

E. The productivity of labour inspectorates

Productivity is usually associated with the private sector, but can also be applied to labour inspectorates.

Productivity is the relationship between what is produced and the resources required to produce it. It is concerned with:

- inputs
- outputs
- the relationship between inputs and outputs.

It is possible to examine a labour inspectorate's productivity by:

- measuring inputs and outputs
- relating inputs and outputs to a definite time-frame.

One measure of productivity is the number of inspections an inspector undertakes monthly or yearly.

> Example:
>
> In a country with 800 inspectors, 32,000 inspections are completed in a year. Each inspector's productivity, on average, is 40 inspections a year, or almost seven every two months.

This measure of productivity does not indicate the quality of inspection work and has the usual distortions of the average as a statistical measure – some inspectors would complete more than seven inspections every two months and some, possibly, none at all.

Despite the simplicity of this measure of productivity, it provides a useful starting point for examining the inspectorate's performance.

- Is seven inspections every two months an acceptable standard?
- Are inspectors, in this case, using their limited time to the best advantage?

Measures other than productivity can be used to review a labour inspectorate's performance.

Example:

Assume, in the above example, that there are 230,000 registered establishments liable to inspection. If 800 inspectors complete 32,000 inspections a year, on average each establishment will be inspected once every seven years.

But if policy dictates that each establishment be inspected once a year, each inspector would have to complete 287 inspections a year or about 24 per month.

- Is this a reasonable standard?
- What needs to be done to increase inspections from seven to 48 every two months?

Raising the level of productivity should not be at the expense of quality. For example it may appear easier to increase the number of inspections by taking short cuts, not undertaking detailed inspections of workplaces, and not writing proper reports.

But it is better to increase productivity by providing:

- improved transport for inspectors
- more and better training
- better office facilities and support equipment.

Improving resource management means giving greater attention to:

- setting inspection targets
- making proper workplans
- monitoring inspectors' performance
- evaluating performance to determine why targets have not been met.

Even where inspectorate staff resources are declining, it is possible to increase productivity by better planning and resource management, and by adopting different methods and approaches for inspection visits.

Example:

If the number of inspectors is reduced by 25 per cent, from 200 to 150, and at the same time the number of inspections falls by 8 per cent, from 25,000 to 23,000, in a given period, productivity has increased from 125 to 153 inspections per inspector. In this case, the number of inspections has decreased but productivity has increased.

Increasing productivity is not a matter of working harder but working smarter.

F. Technological developments

New technological developments make new demands on labour inspection. Examples are:

- industrial robots
- computerized technology
- genetic engineering
- nuclear energy
- new chemicals
- new substances.

New technology requires inspectorates to adapt to a range of **new situations**, including:

- new work processes
- different types of hazards
- new working conditions
- additional work accidents.

New technology – with the potential of major hazards – as used in chemical and nuclear plants, not only affects workers in the immediate working environment but also the population in surrounding areas.

Some of the **implications** of technological developments for labour inspection are given here:

- Which strategies should inspectorates adopt to keep well informed about technological changes and their expected impact?

- How should inspectors' recruitment and training be organized to accommodate new developments?

- How should the inspectorate structure and organization be developed to keep abreast of new technology?

The complexity of the work created by new technologies and the need for **specialist assistance** may involve greater use of external consultants to support mainstream inspectorate staff.

The complexity of technological changes requires placing greater emphasis on labour protection through **prevention** at the earliest possible stage.

More **consultations** are needed before new plants, processes, and chemical substances – which might pose a threat to the safety and health of workers and the wider community – are introduced.

More attention should be given to:

- the study and approval of **factory plans** before construction

- the **centralized inspection** of imported machinery and equipment

- **consultation** with employers and workers on enterprise safety and health prevention policies

- the increased **participation of all parties** in developing a national safety and health policy

- the development of an inspection strategy concentrating on **priority industries and enterprises.**

Employers, workers, and their organizations need to assume more responsibility for workers' protection, with less reliance on the labour inspection service.

G. New work arrangements

Workers' protection is restricted to those covered by collective agreements or those within the legal definitions of 'worker' and 'workplace'.

It is necessary to distinguish between workers protected by the law and those inadequately protected or not protected at all.

Workers with insufficient or no protection include:

- temporary workers
- subcontracted workers
- homeworkers
- rural workers
- urban non-formal-sector workers
- domestic workers
- part-time workers
- women workers
- disabled workers
- child workers
- young workers.

Labour inspectorates, generally, do not adequately serve these categories of workers for various reasons:

- The law may confine their activities to particular categories of workers rather than workers in general.
- Their efforts concentrate on formal wage-sector employment.
- Their efforts focus on groups of workers rather than individuals.

Where certain categories of workers are excluded from protective legislation, inspectorates should bring this to the notice of the authorities concerned with a view to initiating a change in the law to increase its coverage.

Where the law extends coverage to all categories of workers, inspectorates must develop a strategy to ensure that inspection activities do, in fact, extend to **all** such categories.

H. Homeworkers

To reduce costs and improve their competitive position, enterprises are increasingly using work arrangements involving homeworkers.

A homeworker is broadly defined as a person who:

- undertakes work in the home or in premises other than the workplace
- renders a service or makes a product as specified by the employer, irrespective of who provides the equipment or materials.

Homeworkers, like wage earners, are entitled to equality of treatment, for example:

- the right to join trade unions
- protection against discrimination
- work safety and health
- remuneration
- access to training
- maternity rights and benefits
- minimum age provisions.

Inspectorates face difficulty in providing protection to homeworkers because of:

- restrictive legal definitions of 'workers'
- definitions of the 'workplace' which may exclude private homes.

Until the law is changed to allow inspectors improved access to homeworkers, inspectors should use other means (e.g. mass media) to encourage homeworkers to lodge formal complaints, which can then be acted upon by requiring employers to attend the labour office for interviews.

I. Extension of inspection coverage

Extending labour inspection coverage requires considering:

- inspectorates' legal powers
- resource availability
- planning and priorities
- involvement of other agencies
- use of the media.

1. Inspectorates' legal powers

Inspectorates' legal powers may be:

- extensive or
- narrow.

If their legal powers are extensive, they will apply to all workers in all circumstances, including in the:

- formal and non-formal sectors
- commercial and non-commercial sectors
- industrial and non-industrial sectors
- agricultural and non-agricultural sectors
- urban and rural sectors.

Inspectors must ensure their services extend to all workplaces, large and small, in all locations, covering the employed and self-employed.

If their legal powers are very narrow, their work will be confined to providing information and advice rather than undertaking inspection and enforcing the law. In such cases their advice should include efforts to change the law to extend coverage to more workers.

2. Resource availability

Inspectorates could do more if they have additional resources. Their resource situation would improve by:

- making better use of existing resources
- receiving additional or new resources.

Better use of existing resources is not just a matter of inspectors working harder but mainly of inspectorates working harder and smarter through:

- better planning and management
- more motivated inspectors
- stricter performance monitoring.

Obtaining additional resources (staff, vehicles, office equipment) will depend, partly, on inspectorates convincing resource allocators that:

- existing resources are being used efficiently and effectively
- new resources will make a real contribution to national progress.

3. *Planning and priorities*

Improving inspectorates' performance requires reassessing priorities to ensure that limited inspection resources concentrate on high-risk enterprises where safety and health conditions are below standard and the terms and conditions of employment do not meet legal requirements. This requires that inspectorates develop a methodology to determine the degree of risk in each enterprise, based on considerations like:

- size of enterprise
- nature of its processes and products (e.g. use of chemicals and boilers)
- trend in work accidents
- trend in labour disputes
- existence of trade unions
- existence of consultative committees (safety and health committee, joint consultative body)
- work arrangements (contract workers, part-time and casual workers, homeworkers)
- profile of workers (the unskilled, women, young persons, migrants).

4. Involvement of other agencies

Even with additional resources inspectorates will have difficulty in providing services to all workers and all enterprises. Therefore, they should encourage other parties to assume responsibility for some of the functions undertaken by inspectorates, particularly:

- individual employers
- employers' organizations
- trade unions.

Individual employers, both large and small, can do much to encourage greater consultation and discussion with workers on working conditions and the working environment. Inspectorates can advise and encourage employers to form safety and health committees, workers' committees, works committees, joint consultative bodies, and informal work groups to assume responsibility for some of the matters normally undertaken by labour inspectors.

Employers' organizations can be encouraged to advise individual employers on good work practice, and assist them in undertaking more self-inspection, as good work practice is good business.

Trade unions at the industry and enterprise levels can do much to bring breaches of the labour law and regulations to the attention of individual employers and employers' organizations, thereby improving workers' protection. They can also actively encourage and participate in collective bargaining on working conditions and workplace safety and health.

In encouraging employers, employers' organizations, and trade unions to become more involved in labour protection, inspectorates also become more concerned with providing advice on what can be done and how, giving information, and training employers and workers to enable them to participate effectively in self-reliant approaches. Their law-enforcement role, though vital, is of secondary importance.

Although self-reliance in inspection matters is to be actively encouraged, in many enterprises and work situations there are no trade unions, and employers are not sufficiently concerned about workers' protection. These enterprises are often small and located in remote areas not normally visited by labour inspectors. In such cases inspectorates might work more closely with:

- local government agencies
- agricultural extension officers
- business extension officers.

Inspectors can make such agencies and officials aware of the basic aspects of labour protection so that they can pass on this information to workers and employers in an advisory capacity.

In such circumstances inspectors are not delegating their statutory authority to unauthorized persons. They are simply enlisting the support and cooperation of other agencies so that the activities and information services of inspectorates have the widest possible impact.

5. Use of the media

Inspectorates can have better contact with employers, workers, employers' organizations, and trade unions by making use of the mass media and other information channels:

- radio broadcasts
- television announcements
- regular newspaper columns

- news reports in the newsletters and publications of other agencies
- news coverage of special events (e.g. safety campaigns).

Such approaches can bring to employers' and workers' attention their rights and obligations, and the benefits of good work practice, and enable them to obtain more information from inspectorates.

Involving some inspectors in community-outreach and public-relations activities may reduce their involvement in hands-on inspection and law enforcement. But greater use of the media should be seen as an investment leading to increased workers' protection in the future.

Annex

Convention No. 81

Convention concerning Labour Inspection in Industry and Commerce[1]

The General Conference of the International Labour Organization,

Having been convened at Geneva by the Governing Body of the International Labour Office, and having met in its Thirtieth Session on 19 June 1947, and

Having decided upon the adoption of certain proposals with regard to the organization of labour inspection in industry and commerce, which is the fourth item on the agenda of the Session, and

Having determined that these proposals shall take the form of an international Convention,

adopts this eleventh day of July of the year one thousand nine hundred and forty-seven, the following Convention, which may be cited as the Labour Inspection Convention, 1947:

PART I. LABOUR INSPECTION IN INDUSTRY

Article 1

Each Member of the International Labour Organization for which this Convention is in force shall maintain a system of labour inspection in industrial workplaces.

---

[1] Date of coming into force: 7 April 1950,

Article 2

1. The system of labour inspection in industrial workplaces shall apply to all workplaces in respect of which legal provisions relating to conditions of work and the protection of workers while engaged in their work are enforceable by labour inspectors.

2. National laws or regulations may exempt mining and transport undertakings or parts of such undertakings from the application of this Convention.

Article 3

1. The functions of the system of labour inspection shall be:

(a) to secure the enforcement of the legal provisions relating to conditions of work and the protection of workers while engaged in their work, such as provisions relating to hours, wages, safety, health and welfare, the employment of children and young persons, and other connected matters, in so far as such provisions are enforceable by labour inspectors;

(b) to supply technical information and advice to employers and workers concerning the most effective means of complying with the legal provisions;

(c) to bring to the notice of the competent authority defects or abuses not specifically covered by existing legal provisions.

2. Any further duties which may be entrusted to labour inspectors shall not be such as to interfere with the effective discharge of their primary duties or to prejudice in any way the authority and impartiality which are necessary to inspectors in their relations with employers and workers.

Article 4

1. So far as is compatible with the administrative practice of the Member, labour inspection shall be placed under the supervision and control of a central authority.

2. In the case of a federal State, the term "central authority" may mean either a federal authority or a central authority of a federated unit.

Article 5

The competent authority shall make appropriate arrangements to promote:

(a) effective cooperation between the inspection services and other government services and public or private institutions engaged in similar activities; and

(b) collaboration between officials of the labour inspectorate and employers and workers or their organizations.

Article 6

The inspection staff shall be composed of public officials whose status and conditions of service are such that they are assured of stability of employment and are independent of changes of government and of improper external influences.

Article 7

1. Subject to any conditions for recruitment to the public service which may be prescribed by national laws or regulations, labour inspectors shall be recruited with sole regard to their qualifications for the performance of their duties.

2. The means of ascertaining such qualifications shall be determined by the competent authority.

3. Labour inspectors shall be adequately trained for the performance of their duties.

Article 8

Both men and women shall be eligible for appointment to the inspection staff; where necessary, special duties may be assigned to men and women inspectors.

Article 9

Each Member shall take the necessary measures to ensure that duly qualified technical experts and specialists, including specialists in medicine, engineering, electricity and chemistry, are associated in the work of inspection, in such manner as may be deemed most appropriate under national conditions, for the purpose of securing the enforcement of the legal provisions relating to the protection of the health and safety of workers while engaged in their work and of investigating the effects of processes, materials and methods of work on the health and safety of workers.

Article 10

The number of labour inspectors shall be sufficient to secure the effective discharge of the duties of the inspectorate and shall be determined with due regard for:

(a) the importance of the duties which inspectors have to perform, in particular –

   (i) the number, nature, size and situation of the workplaces liable to inspection;

   (ii) the number and classes of workers employed in such workplaces; and

   (iii) the number and complexity of the legal provisions to be enforced;

(b) the material means placed at the disposal of the inspectors; and

(c) the practical conditions under which visits of inspection must be carried out in order to be effective.

Article 11

1. The competent authority shall make the necessary arrangements to furnish labour inspectors with –

(a) local offices, suitably equipped in accordance with the requirements of the service, and accessible to all persons concerned;

(b) the transport facilities necessary for the performance of their duties in cases where suitable public facilities do not exist.

2. The competent authority shall make the necessary arrangements to reimburse to labour inspectors any travelling and incidental expenses which may be necessary for the performance of their duties.

Article 12

1. Labour inspectors provided with proper credentials shall be empowered:

(a) to enter freely and without previous notice at any hour of the day or night any workplace liable to inspection;

(b) to enter by day any premises which they may have reasonable cause to believe to be liable to inspection; and

(c) to carry out any examination, test or enquiry which they may consider necessary in order to satisfy themselves that the legal provisions are being strictly observed, and in particular –

   (i) to interrogate, alone or in the presence of witnesses, the employer or the staff of the undertaking on any matters concerning the application of the legal provisions;

   (ii) to require the production of any books, registers or other documents the keeping of which is prescribed by national laws or regulations relating to conditions of work, in order to see that they are in conformity with the legal provisions, and to copy such documents or make extracts from them;

   (iii) to enforce the posting of notices required by the legal provisions;

(iv) to take or remove for purposes of analysis samples of materials and substances used or handled, subject to the employer or his representative being notified of any samples or substances taken or removed for such purpose.

2. On the occasion of an inspection visit, inspectors shall notify the employer or his representative of their presence, unless they consider that such a notification may be prejudicial to the performance of their duties.

Article 13

1. Labour inspectors shall be empowered to take steps with a view to remedying defects observed in plant, layout or working methods which they may have reasonable cause to believe constitute a threat to the health or safety of the workers.

2. In order to enable inspectors to take such steps they shall be empowered, subject to any right of appeal to a judicial or administrative authority which may be provided by law, to make or to have made orders requiring –

(a) such alterations to the installation or plant, to be carried out within a specified time limit, as may be necessary to secure compliance with the legal provisions relating to the health or safety of the workers; or

(b) measures with immediate executory force in the event of imminent danger to the health or safety of the workers.

3. Where the procedure prescribed in paragraph 2 is not compatible with the administrative or judicial practice of the Member, inspectors shall have the right to apply to the competent authority for the issue of orders or for the initiation of measures with immediate executory force.

Article 14

The labour inspectorate shall be notified of industrial accidents and cases of occupational disease in such cases and in such manner as may be prescribed by national laws or regulations.

Article 15

Subject to such exceptions as may be made by national laws or regulations, labour inspectors –

(a) shall be prohibited from having any direct or indirect interest in the undertakings under their supervision;

(b) shall be bound on pain of appropriate penalties or disciplinary measures not to reveal, even after leaving the service, any manufacturing or commercial secrets or working processes which may come to their knowledge in the course of their duties; and

(c) shall treat as absolutely confidential the source of any complaint bringing to their notice a defect or breach of legal provisions and shall give no intimation to the employer or his representative that a visit of inspection was made in consequence of the receipt of such a complaint.

Article 16

Workplaces shall be inspected as often and as thoroughly as is necessary to ensure the effective application of the relevant legal provisions.

Article 17

1. Persons who violate or neglect to observe legal provisions enforceable by labour inspectors shall be liable to prompt legal proceedings without previous warning: provided that exceptions may be made by national laws or regulations in respect of cases in which previous notice to carry out remedial or preventive measures is to be given.

2. It shall be left to the discretion of labour inspectors to give warning and advice instead of instituting or recommending proceedings.

Article 18

Adequate penalties for violations of the legal provisions enforceable by labour inspectors and for obstructing labour inspectors in the performance of their duties shall be provided for by national laws or regulations and effectively enforced.

Article 19

1. Labour inspectors or local inspection offices, as the case may be, shall be required to submit to the central inspection authority periodical reports on the results of their inspection activities.

2. These reports shall be drawn up in such manner and deal with such subjects as may from time to time be prescribed by the central authority; they shall be submitted at least as frequently as may be prescribed by that authority and in any case not less frequently than once a year.

Article 20

1. The central inspection authority shall publish an annual general report on the work of the inspection services under its control.

2. Such annual reports shall be published within a reasonable time after the end of the year to which they relate and in any case within twelve months.

3. Copies of the annual reports shall be transmitted to the Director-General of the International Labour Office within a reasonable period after their publication and in any case within three months.

Article 21

The annual report published by the central inspection authority shall deal with the following and other relevant subjects in so far as they are under the control of the said authority:

(a) laws and regulations relevant to the work of the inspection service;

(b) staff of the labour inspection service;

(c) statistics of workplaces liable to inspection and the number of workers employed therein;

(d) statistics of inspection visits;

(e) statistics of violations and penalties imposed;

(f) statistics of industrial accidents;

(g) statistics of occupational diseases.

PART II. LABOUR INSPECTION IN COMMERCE

Article 22

Each Member of the International Labour Organization for which this Part of this Convention is in force shall maintain a system of labour inspection in commercial workplaces.

Article 23

The system of labour inspection in commercial workplaces shall apply to workplaces in respect of which legal provisions relating to conditions of work and the protection of workers while engaged in their work are enforceable by labour inspectors.

Article 24

The system of labour inspection in commercial workplaces shall comply with the requirements of Article 3 to 21 of this Convention in so far as they are applicable.

PART III. MISCELLANEOUS PROVISIONS

Article 25

1. Any Member of the International Labour Organization which ratifies this Convention may, by a declaration appended to its ratification, exclude Part II from its acceptance of the Convention.

2. Any Member which has made such a declaration may at any time cancel that declaration by a subsequent declaration.

3. Every Member for which a declaration made under paragraph 1 of this Article is in force shall indicate each year in its annual report upon the application of this Convention the position of its law and practice in regard to the provisions of Part II of this Convention and the extent to which effect has been given, or is proposed to be given, to the said provisions.

Article 26

In any case in which it is doubtful whether any undertaking, part or service of an undertaking or workplace is an undertaking, part, service or workplace to which this Convention applies, the question shall be settled by the competent authority.

Article 27

In this Convention the term "legal provisions" includes, in addition to laws and regulations, arbitration awards and collective agreements upon which the force of law is conferred and which are enforceable by labour inspectors.

Article 28

There shall be included in the annual reports to be submitted under article 22 of the Constitution of the International Labour Organization full information concerning all laws and regulations by which effect is given to the provisions of this Convention.

Article 29

1. In the case of a Member, the territory of which includes large areas where, by reason of the sparseness of the population or the stage of development of the area, the competent authority considers it impracticable to enforce the provisions of this Convention, the authority may exempt such areas from the application of this Convention either generally or with such exceptions in respect of particular undertakings or occupations as it thinks fit.

2. Each Member shall indicate in its first annual report upon the application of this Convention submitted under article 22 of the Constitution of the International Labour Organization any areas in respect of which it proposes to have recourse to the provisions of the present Article and shall give the reasons for which it proposes to have recourse thereto; no Member shall, after the date of its first annual report, have recourse to the provisions of the present Article except in respect of areas so indicated.

3. Each Member having recourse to the provisions of the present Article shall indicate in subsequent annual reports any areas in respect of which it renounces the right to have recourse to the provisions of the present Article.

Article 30

1. In respect of the territories referred to in article 35 of the Constitution of the International Labour Organization as amended by the Constitution of the International Labour Organization Instrument of Amendment, 1946, other than the territories referred to in paragraphs 4 and 5 of the said article as so amended, each Member of the Organization which ratifies this Convention shall communicate to the Director-General of the International Labour Office as soon as possible after ratification a declaration stating –

(a) the territories in respect of which it undertakes that the provisions of the Convention shall be applied without modification;

(b) the territories in respect of which it undertakes that the provisions of the Convention shall be applied subject to modifications, together with details of the said modifications;

(c) the territories in respect of which the Convention is inapplicable and in such cases the grounds on which it is inapplicable;

(d) the territories in respect of which it reserves its decision.

2. The undertakings referred to in subparagraphs (a) and (b) of paragraph 1 of this Article shall be deemed to be an integral part of the ratification and shall have the force of ratification.

3. Any Member may at any time by a subsequent declaration cancel in whole or in part any reservations made in its original declaration in virtue of subparagraphs (b), (c) or (d) of paragraph 1 of this Article.

4. Any Member may, at any time at which the Convention is subject to denunciation in accordance with the provision of Article 34, communicate to the Director-General a declaration modifying in any other respect the terms of any former declaration and stating the present position in respect of such territories as it may specify.

Article 31

1. Where the subject matter of this Convention is within the self-governing powers of any non-metropolitan territory, the Member responsible for the international relations of that territory may, in agreement with the Government of the territory, communicate to the Director-General of the International Labour Office a declaration accepting on behalf of the territory the obligations of this Convention.

2. A declaration accepting the obligations of this Convention may be communicated to the Director-General of the International Labour Office –

(a) by two or more Members of the Organization in respect of any territory which is under their joint authority; or

(b) by any international authority responsible for the administration of any territory, in virtue of the Charter of the United Nations or otherwise, in respect of any such territory.

3. Declarations communicated to the Director-General of the International Labour Office in accordance with the preceding paragraphs of this Article shall indicate whether the provisions of the Convention will be applied in the territory concerned without modification or subject to modifications; when the declaration indicates that the provisions of the Convention will be applied subject to modifications it shall give details of the said modifications.

4. The Member, Members or international authority concerned may at any time by a subsequent declaration renounce in whole or in part the right to have recourse to any modification indicated in any former declaration.

5. The Member, Members or international authority concerned may, at any time at which this Convention is subject to denunciation in accordance with the provisions of Article 34, communicate to the Director-General a declaration modifying in any other respect the terms of any former declaration and stating the present position in respect of the application of the Convention.

PART IV. FINAL PROVISIONS

Article 32

The formal ratifications of this Convention shall be communicated to the Director-General of the International Labour Office for registration.

Article 33

1. This Convention shall be binding only upon those Members of the International Labour Organization whose ratifications have been registered with the Director-General.

2. It shall come into force 12 months after the date on which the ratifications of two Members have been registered with the Director-General.

3. Thereafter, this Convention shall come into force for any Member 12 months after the date on which its ratification has been registered.

Article 34

1. A Member which has ratified this Convention may denounce it after the expiration of ten years from the date on which the Convention first comes into force, by an act communicated to the Director-General of the International Labour Office for registration. Such denunciation shall not take effect until one year after the date on which it is registered.

2. Each Member which has ratified this Convention and which does not, within the year following the expiration of the period of ten years mentioned in the preceding paragraph, exercise the right of denunciation provided for in this Article, will be bound for another period of ten years and, thereafter, may denounce this Convention at the expiration of each period of ten years under the terms provided for in this Article.

Article 35

1. The Director-General of the International Labour Office shall notify all Members of the International Labour Organization of the registration of all ratifications and denunciations communicated to him by the Members of the Organization.

2. When notifying the Members of the Organization of the registration of the second ratification communicated to him, the Director-General shall draw the attention of the Members of the Organization to the date on which the Convention will come into force.

Article 36

The Director-General of the International Labour Office shall communicate to the Secretary-General of the United Nations for registration in accordance with article 102 of the Charter of the United Nations full particulars of all ratifications and acts of denunciation registered by him in accordance with the provisions of the preceding Articles.

Article 37

At such times as it may consider necessary the Governing Body of the International Labour Office shall present to the General Conference a report on the working of this Convention and shall examine the desirability of placing on the agenda of the Conference the question of its revision in whole or in part.

Article 38

1. Should the Conference adopt a new Convention revising this Convention in whole or in part, then, unless the new Convention otherwise provides –

(a) the ratification by a Member of the new revising Convention shall *ipso jure* involve the immediate denunciation of this Convention, notwithstanding the provisions of Article 34 above, if and when the new revising Convention shall have come into force;

(b) as from the date when the new revising Convention comes into force this Convention shall cease to be open to ratification by the Members.

2. This Convention shall in any case remain in force in its actual form and content for those Members which have ratified it but have not ratified the revising Convention.

Article 39

The English and French versions of the text of this Convention are equally authoritative.

Recommendation No. 81

Recommendation concerning Labour Inspection

The General Conference of the International Labour Organization,

Having been convened at Geneva by the Governing Body of the International Labour Office, and having met in its Thirtieth Session on 19 June 1947, and

Having decided upon the adoption of certain proposals with regard to the organization of labour inspection in industry and commerce, which is the fourth item on the agenda of the Session, and

Having determined that these proposals shall take the form of a Recommendation supplementing the Labour Inspection Recommendation, 1923, and the Labour Inspection Convention, 1947,

adopts this eleventh day of July of the year one thousand nine hundred and forty-seven, the following Recommendation, which may be cited as the Labour Inspection Recommendation, 1947:

Whereas the Labour Inspection Recommendation, 1923, and the Labour Inspection Convention, 1947, provide for organization of systems of labour inspection and it is desirable to supplement the provisions thereof by further recommendations;

The Conference recommends that each Member should apply the following provisions as rapidly as national conditions allow and report to the International Labour Office as requested by the Governing Body concerning the measures taken to give effect thereto.

I. PREVENTIVE DUTIES OF LABOUR INSPECTORATES

1. Any person who proposes to open an industrial or commercial establishment, or to take over such an establishment, or to commence in such an establishment the carrying on of a class of activity specified by a competent authority as materially affecting the application of legal provisions enforceable by labour inspectors, should be required to give notice in advance to the competent labour inspectorate either directly or through another designated authority.

2. Members should make arrangements under which plans for new establishments, plant, or processes of production may be submitted to the appropriate labour inspection service for an opinion as to whether the said plans would render difficult or impossible compliance with the laws and regulations concerning industrial health and safety or would be likely to constitute a threat to the health or safety of the workers.

3. Subject to any right of appeal which may be provided by law, the execution of plans for new establishments, plant and processes of production deemed under national laws or regulation to be dangerous or unhealthy should be conditional upon the carrying out of any alterations ordered by the inspectorate for the purpose of securing the health and safety of the workers.

II. COLLABORATION OF EMPLOYERS AND WORKERS IN REGARD TO HEALTH AND SAFETY

4. (1) Arrangements for collaboration between employers and workers for the purpose of improving conditions affecting the health and safety of the workers should be encouraged.

(2) Such arrangements might take the form of safety committees or similar bodies set up within each undertaking or establishment and including representatives of the employers and the workers.

5. Representatives of the workers and the management, and more particularly members of works safety committees or similar bodies where such exist, should be authorized to collaborate directly with officials of the labour inspectorate, in a manner and within limits fixed by the competent authority, when investigations and, in particular, enquiries into industrial accidents or occupational diseases are carried out.

6. The promotion of collaboration between officials of the labour inspectorate and organizations of employers and workers should be facilitated by the organization of conferences or joint committees, or similar bodies, in which representatives of the labour inspectorate discuss with representatives of organizations of employers and workers questions concerning the enforcement of labour legislation and the health and safety of the workers.

7. Appropriate steps should be taken to ensure that employers and workers are given advice and instruction in labour legislation and questions of industrial hygiene and safety by such measures as:

(a) lectures, radio talks, posters, pamphlets and films explaining the provisions of labour legislation and suggesting methods for their application and measures for preventing industrial accidents and occupational diseases;

(b) health and safety exhibitions; and

(c) instruction in industrial hygiene and safety in technical schools.

III. LABOUR DISPUTES

8. The functions of labour inspectors should not include that of acting as conciliator or arbitrator in proceedings concerning labour disputes.

IV. ANNUAL REPORTS ON INSPECTION

9. The published annual reports on the work of inspection services should, in so far as possible, supply the following detailed information:

(a) a list of the laws and regulations bearing on the work of the inspection system not mentioned in previous reports;

(b) particulars of the staff of the labour inspection system, including:

  (i) the aggregate number of inspectors;

  (ii) the numbers of inspectors of different categories;

  (iii) the number of women inspectors; and

  (iv) particulars of the geographical distribution of inspection services;

(c) statistics of workplaces liable to inspection and of the number of persons therein employed, including:

  (i) the number of workplaces liable to inspection;

  (ii) the average number of persons employed in such workplaces during the year;

  (iii) particulars of the classification of persons employed under the following headings: men, women, young persons, and children;

(d) statistics of inspection visits, including:

(i) the number of workplaces visited;

(ii) the number of inspection visits made, classified according to whether they were made by day or by night;

(iii) the number of persons employed in the workplaces visited;

(iv) the number of workplaces visited more than once during the year;

(e) statistics of violations and penalties, including:

(i) the number of infringements reported to the competent authorities;

(ii) particulars of the classification of such infringements according to the legal provisions to which they relate;

(iii) the number of convictions;

(iv) particulars of the nature of the penalties imposed by the competent authorities in the various cases (fines, imprisonment, etc.);

(f) statistics of industrial accidents, including the number of industrial accidents notified and particulars of the classification of such accidents:

(i) by industry and occupation;

(ii) according to cause;

(iii) according to whether fatal or non-fatal;

(g) statistics of occupational diseases, including:

   (i) the number of cases of occupational disease notified;

   (ii) particulars of the classification of such cases according to industry and occupation;

   (iii) particulars of the classification of such cases according to their cause or character, such as the nature of the disease, poisonous substance or unhealthy process to which the disease is due.

www.ingramcontent.com/pod-product-compliance
Ingram Content Group UK Ltd.
Pitfield, Milton Keynes, MK11 3LW, UK
UKHW041850190726
13854UKWH00002B/803

9 789221 112808